Swedish Trivia Book

Interesting and Fun Facts
About Swedish Culture,
History, Tourist Attractions,
and Much More

Alex Anderson

Contents

Introduction

Do you know some indisputable benefits of engaging with trivia about things, people, countries, and everything else?

Trivia builds brain muscle which, in turn, enhances mental strength.

Trivia is fun, reduces stress and anxiety, and expands your mind. You can see beyond your life and belief systems, giving you the mental width to accept much more than what your life gives you.

You become interesting when you rattle off random, not-so-well facts in a social gathering, and more people will flock toward you. Not only that, when you answer trivia questions, you feel really good about yourself.

Usually, trivia games and quizzes are played with time constraints. The more you play, the more you exercise your brain to work under pressure. Therefore, trivia helps you improve your working capabilities under pressure.

The more you read trivia, the more your memory power improves. Trivia is often linked to interesting, sometimes weird, information that is not easily forgettable. As you connect with trivia more, your mind finds different methods to remember and recall other facts, boosting your memory skills.

So, why should you spend your time on this Swedish trivia book?

Well, Sweden is one of the most beautiful and ancient countries of Scandinavia, filled with interesting tidbits that are easy to read and recall and talk about to pep up the atmosphere in social gatherings.

This book is a one-stop shop for Swedish trivia. It's divided into four broad categories:

- Swedish culture and society.
- Swedish history.
- Swedish geography.
- Trivia about Swedish tourist attractions (perfect for you if you plan to visit Sweden!).

Every category is filled with interesting and

unforgettable stories and ends with a "ten interesting facts about"-section.

Enjoy the book, and don't forget to take the Swedish quiz at the end!

1. Swedish Culture and Society

The Swedish pride themselves on creating one of the most egalitarian societies in the modern world, a society founded on individualism and equality. Their commitment to environmental sustainability is commendable, with Sweden being a world leader in recycling, organic agriculture, and renewable energy.

The Swedes believe in the balance of everything and have a word to describe this philosophical facet, **Lagom.** Lagom means "not too much, not too little, just right…" They value humility, integrity, and honesty above all else. Initially, the Swedes might come across as being shy and reserved. In reality, they are very friendly and caring and have a great sense of humor.

"Lagom" Has No English Equivalent

"Lagom" loosely stands for moderation and balance and is an inherent quality of Swedish society. However, it goes deeper and wider than moderation. The concept of "Lagom" can go something like "the right amount, neither more nor less, is the best" or "having enough is as good as having a grand feast."

"Lagom" underpins contentment and reflects all aspects of Swedish society, including laws, architecture, and more. For example, tax-funded government schemes are based on the belief that everyone should have enough, and no one should be without. Swedish architecture is based on functionality, simplicity, and effective use of natural resources without going overboard. Even Swedish cuisine revolves around simplicity and "being enough." "Lagom" is the absence of flashiness and excess of any kind.

Freedom to Roam

The Swedes' commitment to environmental sustainability is rooted in their immense love for nature. You will often find that plenty of Swedes spend their leisure either by the sea or in a forest. Sweden's Right to Public Access or Outdoor Access ('Allemansrätten') gives you complete freedom and the right to travel through and roam the countryside in peace and quiet.

Called "Freedom to Roam," this unique law gives you the right to walk, cycle, ride, camp, or ski on any public land to soak in the beauty of Sweden's nature. You are allowed to pick mushrooms, flowers, and berries. Fishing is freely allowed along the coastline and in the five big lakes. You can swim in public lakes and access all beaches. Spaces belonging to private residences, space around 70 meters around a dwelling house, and cultivated land are restricted from this right.

No Shoes Allowed Indoors

The Swedes do not wear shoes in their homes. Therefore, if you visit the home of a Swede, remember to remove your footwear and place it in the designated stand, usually near the main door. Interestingly, the removal of footwear is mandatory before entering homes and schools.

This cultural idea is likely to be founded on the fact that coming inside with your shoes on will bring in icy puddles or slushy snow, dirtying the home. This rule is followed throughout the year, but especially in winter. Some people tend to carry a clean pair of footwear, specifically for indoor use. The rule followed in schools has a related interesting ten-year study (at the University of Bournemouth) that showed children without shoes tend to behave better and learn better than those with shoes.

Valborg - The Start of Warm, Sunny Weather

Valborg is an old tradition celebrated on April 30, coinciding with the king's birthday. In the olden days, it was a day when large bonfires were lit, and a lot of noise was made to scare off evil witches and bad spirits. Today, Valborg is a day of celebration to usher in warm, sunny weather that usually comes in May and to say goodbye to the cold, uncertain climates of April.

Valborg, also called Walpurgis, is a community festival, not a family one. The day usually starts with a breakfast of strawberries and champagne. The young Swedes mostly participate in music and river rafting competitions. Older people generally tend to focus on cultural events that happen all over the country during Valborg.

Midsummer

Midsummer is a summer solstice celebration and a cherished Swedish tradition. It is celebrated on a Friday between the 19th and 25th of June every year. In cold climes like Sweden, long, sunny days are rare. The summer solstice is the longest day of the year and is, therefore, celebrated with gusto.

Interestingly, during Midsummer, the Swedes travel to the countryside with their families, and the urban areas become quiet. However, midsummer festivities are held all over Sweden. This festive day is marked by never-ending lunch parties and involves wearing flowers in your hair, guzzling schnapps, pole dancing, and singing songs. The best place for Midsummer is Riksgränsen, Swedish Lapland, where the sun never sets at this time of the year.

Lucia and Christmas in Sweden

"Jul" is Christmas in Sweden! When in Sweden, you say "God Jul," which is Merry Christmas. The Swedes celebrate Christmas like the rest of the world, except for a few unique things.

On December 13 every year, as part of the Christmas celebrations, people line up outside churches to watch a parade of girls dressed in white robes, holding candles, and singing songs. One of the girls wears a crown and holds the candle on her head, playing the role of Santa Lucia, the Saint of Light. Many young Swedish girls dream of playing Santa Lucia.

A mulled wine called Glögg, made with fragrant spices is the highlight of Swedish Christmas. Before you drink it, you add raisins and almond slices which are fished out using a small spoon to be eaten.

Free Education

In Sweden, education is free and compulsory. Children go to school for at least 10 years from age six. Compulsory schooling consists of four stages, namely:

- *Förskoleklass* ('preschool year' or year 0)

- *Lågstadiet* (years 1–3)

- *Mellanstadiet* (years 4–6)

- *Högstadiet* (years 7–9).

Also, compulsory schooling includes a school (called Sameskolor) for the indigenous Sami people. Education covers all genders and races and learning capabilities. The upper secondary school, gymnasium, is optional, and you can choose between courses for vocational training and to get into higher academics.

Religion in Sweden

Sweden is a secular country, and the Church of Sweden (professing to be a part of the Lutheran branch) was separated from the state in 2000. Religion and the state are disconnected and mutually exclusive. But religion still plays a big role in Swedish society, mostly through religious rituals, primarily weddings, christenings, and funerals, all of which are conducted with zest and gusto.

Nearly half of the priests in the Church of Sweden are women. Same-sex marriages began to be solemnized in churches in the same year they were legalized in the country, viz 2009.

Child-Friendly (Compensation When Your Child Is Sick)

The Swedes take their children and child care very seriously, not limited to free education. The entire landscape of cities and urban areas is made child-friendly. Playgrounds and parks have ramps for prams. Nearly all libraries, restaurants, and shopping areas have nursing and diaper-changing stations and sections. All restaurants provide high chairs for toddlers and kids.

If you are a parent working in Sweden and need a few days off to take care of a sick child, you are covered and compensated by the Swedish Social Insurance Agency, which is available for working parents with children younger than 12 years of age. Compensation is available for children between 12 and 15 years of age when a doctor's certificate is produced.

Sweden Is Folkhemmet

Folkhemmet means "the people's home." This term is a metaphor to describe Sweden as a country household, similar to a family household wherein every member cares for and loves every other member as their own. In addition to mutual care and concern, the Swedes believe in democratic qualities of equality and dignity for all. Swedish society is founded on the basis of social welfare. Free education, the importance of child welfare, tax-funded health care, and more such elements reflect the egalitarianism of Sweden.

Personal Space Is Paramount

While Swedes might appear to be shy and reserved, the true reason for their reticent behavior, especially in public, is their respect for others' personal space. The personal space of every individual is honored and respected. This is why people use hushed tones to speak in public, keep a minimum physical distance from others, and minimize physical contact.

For example, it is rare for a Swede to sit next to a stranger on public transport or talk to strangers without rhyme or reason. The Swedes also do not divulge a lot of personal information, opinions, and views in their first meetings with people.

The Swedish "Varsågod"

Varsågod is a Swedish word that translates to "You're welcome." But the word is used in many contexts as a polite phrase, such as:

- If someone says thank you, you can respond with *Varsågod.*

- If you want to pass something on to someone, you can say *Varsågod* (here you go) and pass it.

- The word can be used instead of "please" because there is no Swedish equivalent of, please. So, it can be used to say, "Varsågod och…" which means "please be kind so to."

Varsågod is the formal form, and *Varsågoda* is the plural form.

The Swedish Gift-Giving and Gift-Taking Etiquette

There are special points to remember when giving gifts in Swedish society. Here are some pointers:

- You must carry a small gift for your host/hostess as a token of gratitude for the invitation. It can be something small, a box of chocolates, a bottle of wine, or flowers.

- If it's flowers, then make sure the bouquet does not have chrysanthemums or white lilies because they are used specifically in funerals.

- Taking gifts for the host/hostess' children will get you brownie points, considering that the Swedes value their children so much.

- If you get a gift, then you must open it as soon as you receive it.

The Swedes Do Not Demonstrate Emotions that much

Whether in a personal or professional environment, Swedes do not normally demonstrate emotions. They are cool and calm and rarely get flustered, and even if they do, they are good at hiding it. The showing of emotions is perceived as somewhat negatively by the Swedes.

Moreover, the egalitarian nature imbibed in Swedish culture means all decisions are arrived at only after a consensus is reached. Therefore, not only would it be foolhardy if you tried to endear yourself or impress a senior or elderly person, but your behavior will also be frowned upon. Just talk sensibly and with little or no emotion, especially during negotiations and professional meetings.

Ten Interesting Facts about Swedish Culture and Society

1. Being punctual is vital for the Swedes. You have to come just before time but not very early.

2. Forming an orderly line is imperative in Swedish society. Breaking lines is frowned upon.

3. It is customary to take a small thank-you gift when you are invited to a Swede's home for lunch or dinner.

4. The Swedes love their "Fika," or coffee break, usually accompanied by sandwiches, biscuits, or cinnamon buns.

5. Sweden has a constitutional monarchy form of government where the elected parliament and government hold power while the monarch has ceremonial duties only.

6. Meatballs served with potatoes, and lingonberries are a national dish, a staple meal served in nearly all homes across Sweden.

7. Sweden was the first country to make it illegal to hit children.

8. The Swedes never take hospitality for granted, and kindness is always rewarded with heartfelt gratitude.

9. The Swedes work hard but not excessively hard. They have fun but do not indulge in anything excessive.

10. You must dress smartly when invited to anything by a Swede. Not dressing well is seen as disrespectful to the hosts.

2. Swedish History

The history of Sweden (with sufficient evidence) dates back to the Stone Age, circa 8000 BCE. The region around present-day Sweden was inhabited by our cavemen ancestors who used simple stone tools for hunting, gathering, and fishing. Ample archeological evidence of graves and dwelling places have been and continue to be excavated.

The Sami are believed to be one of the world's oldest indigenous tribes. They are mentioned in one of Sweden's oldest texts, dated around 2000 BCE. More than 2500 rune stones, some of them dating back to the 5th Century, have been found. These runes are considered to be the oldest records of Swedish history.

The Vikings traded with the Arab and Byzantine empires, and modern-day Swedes are actually descendants of the Vikings. Christianity made an entry into Sweden during the 9th Century. It took two centuries before the entire region became Christianized.

The Viking Period

The glory days of the Vikings lasted between 800 and 1050 CE. A flurry of expansion activities by the Vikings characterizes this period. The Vikings set off from Sweden to trade and conquer and annex new territories along the Baltic, reaching as far east as present-day Russia.

The Vikings cruised along the Baltic coast on their flatboats, landed wherever they pleaded, plundered, looted, and took whatever they wanted, including jewelry, food, women and children, and everything and everyone they fancied. Sadly, the only thing the Vikings left behind were chaos, humiliation, death, and destruction.

Sweden - Established in 1164

In 1164, Sweden, or Svea Rike as it was officially named then, became a Catholic archbishopric. The archbishop was seated at Old Uppsala. Svea Rike became the present-day Sverige or Sweden. During the 13th Century, Finland was conquered and merged into Sweden, thanks to the Swedes' military strength and naval power.

The Kalmar Union 1397 - 1523

In the Kalmar Union, the three nations, Sweden, Denmark, and Norway, were united as one under one monarch. However, the Danes did not like this union resulting in a bloody war called Stockholm Bloodbath between the Swedes and the Danes. The Danes won the war but not before killing thousands of Swedes in the central marketplace of Stockholm under the guise of ridding the Kalmar Union of heretics who stood against the Roman Catholic Church. The Stockholm Bloodbath was the beginning of the end of the Kalmar Union.

Gustav Vasa - Sweden's Founding Father

The Stockholm Bloodbath left the Swedes fuming for revenge and liberation. Gustav Vasa, in 1523, led a revolution against the sitting Danish King (who ruled over Sweden at that time) and liberated Sweden from Denmark. Further, Catholicism also lost its sway over Sweden, and the Swedes adopted Protestantism as their state religion. Gustav Vasa is called the Founding Father of Modern Sweden. He died in 1560.

Gustav Adolf II - The One Who Made Sweden "Stormakt"

Gustav Adolf ruled Sweden between 1611 and 1632, during which time he led many expansionist wars with the neighboring countries. Sweden became a powerful nation because of Gustav Adolf II's efforts and declared itself "stormakt," which translates to "great power." He died in battle, leaving behind a daughter, Kristina

Kristina - the Queen of Sweden

Kristina ruled Sweden between 1632 and 1654. Unlike her father, she did not fight battles.

Instead, she converted to Catholicism. She finally gave up her throne, moved to Rome, and dedicated her life to the Roman Catholic Church. She is one of the very few women buried in the Vatican Grotto.

Treaty of Roskilde

The Treaty of Roskilde and the Copenhagen Treaty set the boundaries for present-day Sweden, Norway, and Denmark. It was the culmination of the Second Northern War between Charles X of Sweden and Frederick III of Denmark. Charles Gustav X defeated the Danish army and freed Sweden completely from Danish rule once and for all.

The Treaty of Roskilde was drafted in 1658, by which Sweden acquired the four provinces, including Skåne, Halland, Blekinge, and Bohuslän. The Copenhagen Treaty gave Trondelag to Norway and Bornholm to Denmark, thereby permanently fixing the boundaries of the three countries up until today.

The Freedom of Press Act - 1766

Sweden was the first country to pass the Freedom of Press and Information Act. It was passed on December 2, 1766, by the Swedish Parliament. This act was way ahead of its time and entailed the abolishment of censorship on all printed publications. This law covered even publications imported from other countries. The only restriction to the Freedom of Press Act was theological and academic subjects.

The Freedom of Press Act included the Right to Information to the public wherein Swedish citizens were given access to documents written and drawn up by government agencies. But, severe punishments for anti-government and anti-king writings were not abolished.

Finnish War

The *Finska kriget*, or the Finnish War, was part of the Napoleonic Wars and took place between 1808 and 1809. It was fought between Sweden and the Russian Empire. Sweden lost this war, yet the lessons the Swedes learned from it led them to many excellent reforms, especially within the Swedish bureaucracy.

The rich, elite Swedes understood that the deep corruption within their bureaucracy was one of the biggest contributors to their loss in the Finnish War. The Swedes woke up to this and brought out multiple reformations, setting the trend for the modern, egalitarian society that Sweden is known for today.

The House of Bernadotte

The House of Bernadotte was founded in 1818 and has since remained in Sweden's royal family. Charles XIV John founded the House of Bernadotte. After the Finnish War, Sweden's House of Holstein-Gottorp was declining, and the last king did not have an heir.

The Swedish Parliament decided to choose a king who would have the approval of Napoleon I of France, the emperor who controlled most of Europe at that time. In 1810, the Parliament appointed Jean Baptiste Jules Bernadotte, a powerful French general in Napoleon's army, as the heir presumptive, taking on the title of Prince Bernadotte.

Migration in Sweden

The country has a long, wonderful history of migration, both inward and outward. Merchant trading communities moved from Germany to Sweden in early times and are believed to be the largest immigrant group in the country. The Roma started moving into Sweden in the 1500s. Walloons from Belgium started coming to Sweden around the 1600s and brought their ironsmith skills to the country.

The Jews started arriving in the 1700s. French intellectuals and artisans also accompanied the Jew migration into Sweden, followed by the Italians, who brought their bricklaying and stucco work skills.

From 1850 to 1930, there came about what is today known as "The Great Emigration." During this time, the Swedes migrated to Australia and the Americas for various reasons including:

- In search of greener pastures.

- To escape from religious persecution.

- Fearing no future for the country.

- In anticipation of being part of the "gold rush."

The year 1887 saw the maximum exodus, with over 50,000 Swedes leaving their homeland.

The World Wars

Sweden was more or less a neutral onlooker during both World Wars. The country managed not to enter the war fray at all. However, depending on the situation and its own needs, Sweden chose to sometimes side with the Allies and sometimes with Germany, especially during WW2.

Initially, during WW2, Sweden was neutral, although she favored Germany slightly. But when Germany attacked Denmark and Norway, the country was surrounded by the Nazis. Thanks to the British-imposed sea blockade, Sweden had no choice but to depend on Germany to procure their necessities. The country was forced to allow Germans to use their railroad and even gave military help.

But when the Allies defeated Germany in two important battles between 1942 and 1943, the Swedes could get out of the Nazi stranglehold and tip their support away from the Germans and towards the Allies. Further, Sweden opened its door to Jewish refugees.

Assassination of Prime Minister Olof Palme (1927-1986)

Prime Minister Olof Palme of Sweden is perhaps one of the most controversial leaders of all time. His speeches and ideas were polarizing both within Sweden and internationally. He openly spoke against the world superpowers of that time, namely The Soviet Union and the USA. He supported third-world countries, both vocally and economically. He was one of the first leaders of the Western world to support the Cuban revolutionaries.

Prime Minister Olof Palme was assassinated in February 1986, the first Swedish national leader to be assassinated after Gustav III, way back in 1792.

His death created a huge impact throughout Scandinavia. Many were tried for the assassination, but the murderer's identity is still a mystery in Sweden.

The Swedish Parliament

The Riksdagen is the highest decision-making body in Sweden, covering the country's law-making and budgetary decisions. This assembly also examines the government's works, documents, and other functionalities.

The history of the Swedish Riksdag or Swedish Parliament goes as far back as 1435 when a meeting referred to as the Arboga meeting was called for in Arboga, a little Swedish town. Therefore, many Swedes believe this to be the first parliament in Sweden.

However, it was not until the early 1600s, under the reign of King Gustav Vasa; the Riksdag had representatives from all four estates, including the Nobility, the Clergy, the Burghers, and the Peasantry. The term "Riksdag" was used for the first time in the 1540s. Today, the members of the Swedish Parliament are democratically elected representatives.

No Wars in Sweden

Sweden has not actively participated in any military conflict since 1814 and chose to take a non-confrontational stance to maintain peace and harmony in the entire Scandinavian region, which continues to this day. However, the country does have an active military. The absence of war can be translated as the absence of civil wars, active participation in global wars, military coups, and political violence too. The Swedes realized the folly of war and the humility and wisdom of peaceful measures.

Ten Interesting Facts about Swedish History

1. Multiple useful household items that are taken for granted today, such as the adjustable wrench, zip, oat milk, three-point seat belts, and zip, are Swedish inventions.

2. The Swedish passport is one of the most powerful and accepted passports in the world, allowing you to enter more than 120 countries without a visa.

3. Sweden is home to some of the biggest and best musicians in the world, including ABBA, Ace of Base, Robyn, The Cardigans, and many more.

4. Sweden is the 6th oldest European country with a 1000-year history.

5. At the peak of their military power, the Swedes built a gigantic warship called The

Vasa. This ship was so large and heavy that it sank on its maiden voyage (in 1628), just a mile out into the sea.

6. The ancient vessel has been excavated and reconstructed and finds a pride of place in the Vasa Museum.

7. The capital city of Sweden, Stockholm, was founded in the 13th Century. It was established on Stadsholmen Island, the present-day Old Town. Defensive walls of brick and stone were built for its protection.

8. Stockholm played host to the 1912 Olympic Games, in which 2400 sportspeople from 28 countries participated.

9. Sweden is the birthplace of many global tech and manufacturing companies, including IKEA, Ericsson, Volvo, H&M, Electrolux, and Spotify.

10. Nicotine replacement gum was invented in Sweden.

3. Swedish Geography

Sweden's topography is primarily formed from and by ice. During the previous Ice Age, the Scandinavian region was covered in thick layers of ice which began to melt around 6000 BCE to form coastlines in the southern parts filled with islands, lakes, and streams. The abundance of water and silt from the melting gave rise to thick, green forests in Sweden.

Located in the Scandinavian region of Northern Europe, Sweden is home to lush, green forests and nearly 100,000 lakes. The country is about 1572 km long and is bounded by Norway on the west and Finland on the east. Three straits separate Denmark and Sweden, including the Skagerrak, the Kattegat, and the Öresund Straits.

The northern part of Sweden is often referred to as the "land of the midnight sun," thanks to the geographical phenomenon wherein the sun never sets during the summer months here. In Stockholm, the summer nights usually last only for about four hours, and even during these four hours, it's mostly twilight. During winters, the nights are long, and the days are very, very short.

Aurora Borealis

Aurora Borealis, or the Northern Lights, dance over our heads in the Swedish skies after dark. While it is found a lot in Norway, it is commonly seen in Sweden too. No two sightings are the same. Some people have come away feeling totally underwhelmed, while it has been a life-changing sight for many others. The Northern Lights phenomenon is caused by the disturbances between the sun and the earth's magnetic field. Although they are visible only in the dark, this phenomenon can take place at any time.

According to Norse mythology, the Aurora Borealis (the green lights, specifically) is the pathway through which fallen heroes are taken to Valhalla. Some people believe that these stunning lights are the harbingers of bad news. For example, some Europeans believe that the Aurora Borealis "blazed red" before the bloody French Revolution. The French and Italians also believe these lights are a bad omen and can bring bad luck in the form of wars and plagues.

Sweden's Rivers

Sweden has three primary rivers, namely the Ume, Torne, and the Angerman, all of which flow into the Gulf of Bothnia. River Ume is about 460 km in length, starting its journey to the Gulf of

Bothnia from Lake Overuman. The Ume River is used extensively for hydroelectric power.

River Torne originates in Lake Tornetrask near the Norwegian border. It is approximately 522 km long before it flows into the Gulf of Bothnia. River Angerman is about 460 km long, with its source in the Scandinavian mountain range. It derives its name from Angermanland, the province in which the river is most powerful. It empties into the Gulf of Bothnia near Kramfors town.

The Three Regions of Sweden

Geographically, Sweden can be divided into three regions, namely:

1. **Central and southern Sweden** - Winters are quite cold and short in this region. Summers have a lot more sunshine than other parts of the country.

2. **Northeast Sweden** - In this region, winters are long and severe. Summers are surprisingly warm.

3. **Northwest Sweden** - This region which lies in the far north, has snow all year round on elevated areas. Summers are short, and the summer climes are unpredictable. In nearly all parts of

Sweden, there are long days in summer and long nights in the winter months.

Languages in Sweden

Sweden has one official language and multiple minor languages. Moreover, the immigrants into the country have also brought in their own tongues, all of which (around 200 in number) have now been imbibed into the country's warm embrace. Although the official language of Sweden is Swedish, which is spoken by the majority of Swedes, many speak fluent English also.

The Swedish language is a North Germanic language similar to Danish and Norwegian. Other languages of Sweden include Romani, the Sami languages, Meankieli, Finnish, and Yiddish. While it is possible to get by in Sweden with only English, it is far more convenient to learn Swedish as well.

The Kolen Mountains

The Kolen Mountains in Sweden are part of the larger Scandinavian Mountain Range. These mountains form the border between Sweden and Norway. The eastern range of the Kolen Mountains, called Kebnekaise, is situated in the Swedish Lapland. Kebnekaise has many peaks reaching up to 6500 feet. The highest peak in

Sweden is Mount Kebne which is 6926 feet in height. Kebnekaise is a Sami word that means "kettle top."

Kebnekaise is a climbing haunt during summers and a skiing haunt during winters. The first climb to the summit expedition happened on August 22, 1883, under the leadership of Charles Rabot. However, the first Swedish expedition under Johan Alfred Bjorling is more well-known and received more media attention than the French-led 1883 summit.

21 Swedish Counties or Ian

Sweden is divided into 21 counties. Alphabetically, these 21 counties are Blekinge, Dalarna, Gavleborg, Gotland, Halland, Jamtland, Jonkoping, Kalmar, Kronoberg, Norrbotten, Orebro, Ostergotland, Skane, Sodermanland, Stockholm, Uppsala, Varmland, Vasterbotten, Vasternorrland, Vastmanland and Vastra Gotaland.

Every county has a government-appointed governor who is the head of the county administrative board, which manages and supervises the local administration, especially concerning public transport, healthcare, and local culture.

Stockholm - Sweden's Capital

As mentioned in Chapter Two, the foundations of modern-day Stockholm were laid in the 13th Century when brick and stone walls were built for its defense. However, it must be remembered that people have been living in this area since the Stone Age.

Today, Stockholm is often called "the world's smallest big city" or "the world's biggest small town." This city is an entity by itself and has its own history. Stockholm's subway is known as the world's longest art gallery, and all the subway stations are filled with sculptures, paintings, and other artworks.

Thanks to its beautiful buildings and architecture, Stockholm is also referred to as the " "Venice of the North."

Stockholm - Changed Completely during the 16th Century

During the 16th Century, Sweden was at the peak of its power. Thanks to this, Stockholm also underwent tremendous change. First, the nation converted to Protestant Lutheranism. A lot more stone constructions and buildings came up with the money that new taxes brought for the kings. Stockholm has been the capital of Stockholm since 1523.

People began to move from rural areas of Sweden to Stockholm, and urbanization speeded up. Yet, the worst happened during the 16th Century, the Stockholm Bloodbath, which brought in its wake life lessons that the Swedes never forgot. Corruption, which was rampant until then, was completely eliminated. The Swedes obtained unconditional independence from then on, and Stockholm began to develop and grow. Today, it is the largest Nordic city.

Forests Bathing in Sweden

Nearly half of Sweden is wilderness. Most of the population is concentrated in the southern parts of the country. About 83% of these forests are coniferous. Forest bathing is a thing in Sweden and is called "skogsbad", a word added to the Swedish dictionary recently. Forest bathing has its origins in Japan but found its way into Sweden, thanks to the country's abundance of forest reserves. Sweden is now a forest bathing paradise.

Forest bathing, also called forest therapy, in Sweden comes with a variety of activities, including bird watching, berry picking, swimming in the wild, kayaking excursions, and simple but relaxing hikes in the forests. The most popular forests in Sweden are:

- **Kolmården** - This forest is a long, rocky ridge with dense foliage and separates the provinces of Sodermanland and Ostergotland, two of the main agricultural areas in the country.

- **Tiveden** - The Tiveden is notorious as a hiding place for outlaws right through the history of Sweden. It is infamous for its dangerous wilderness. Today, the Tiveden National Park holds one of the most inaccessible forest areas in the entire country.

- **Tylöskog** - Located in southeast Sweden, Tylöskog is a densely forested area between Ostergotland and Narke (now Orebro) counties.

- **Kilsbergen** - This mountainous, forested ridge separates Orebro from Varmland. The flora and fauna in these forests are unusual for that latitude. It is also known for its elk population.

- **Ed Forest** - This forest separates the Swedish county of Varmland from Norway. Ed Forest is best known for its pilgrimage path leading to Nidaros Cathedral in Trondheim.

Swedish Lakes

The four largest lakes in Sweden are Hjälmaren, Malaren, Vanern, and Vattern.

<u>Lake Hjälmaren</u> - Lake Hjälmaren is very close to Stockholm and is a popular getaway spot for urban vacationers. Fields and forests surround this lake, and protruding rocks and thick vegetation make this lake ideal for game fish, especially pike.

<u>Lake Malaren</u> - The English name of Lake Malaren is Lake Malar, and it is situated west of Stockholm. Originally, Lake Malar was part of the Baltic Sea, but with receding sea levels, it became permanently landlocked into a separate lake between the 10th and 11th centuries. Soon, the separation from the sea was complete, with freshwater from the melting glaciers replacing the salt water.

<u>Lake Vänern</u> - Lake Vänern's shores are dotted with castles dating back to the 13th Century, and it is the largest lake in Sweden. Multiple interlocking locks and canals were built in the 1800s to facilitate inland water transport through Lake Vänern. Today, Lake Vänern offers some spectacular sunrises and sunsets.

<u>Lake Vättern</u> - Most Swedes believe Lake Vättern to be the most scenic of all Swedish lakes, replete with patches of farmland, white sandy beaches,

and beautiful lighthouses. The Town of Hjo on the western banks of Lake Vättern is built entirely of wood and is a reminder of Swedish old-world charm. Lake Vättern is centrally located, giving it easy accessibility too.

Mountain Peaks in Sweden

There are beautiful mountain peaks in Sweden, each offering stunning views and excellent walking trails. The top 7 viewing peaks in Sweden are:

<u>Mount Skierfe</u> - This is located in the Sarek National Park in the Swedish Lapland. It is best known for the views and landscapes it offers of the Rapaalv River.

<u>Gipfel des Städjan</u> - From the summit of this peak (an unremarkable and inconspicuous pile of stones), you can view the skiing paths of Idre Fjäll, a famous winter sports resort in Sweden. You can also see the mountains of Norway from here.

<u>Nuolja</u> - You can walk up this mountain peak or take the chairlift. The summit gives you a spectacular view of Lapporten and the landscapes of Tornetrask.

<u>Gipfel des Storvätteshågna</u> - The summit of this peak gives you amazing views of the Scandinavian wilderness. You also get an unhindered view of a chain of lakes in Tofsingdalen National Park. This peak is the highest one in the Svealand region.

40

Åreskutan - This peak is home to the highest cafe in Sweden. You can use the cable car to ride up to the summit of this mountain or take a short hike with breathtaking views.

Wildlife of Sweden

If more than half of the country is made of forests and jungles, there's no doubt wildlife would be found in plenty, too, in Sweden. This country is home to several species of wolves, lynxes, and brown bears. Here are some of the most wonderful wildlife animals found in Sweden:

Reindeer - Reindeer can be found in abundance in the northern parts of Sweden and in Lapland. Although they might appear to be wild animals roaming freely, the reindeer are almost always partly domesticated and are owned by someone, usually the Sami. Reindeer herding is one of the most common occupations of the Sami people.

Arctic Fox - This endangered species lives in little fragmented herds in the Scandinavian mountains. They need extreme cold for their survival. With climate change, the arctic foxes are being hunted by the Red Fox, whose population is surging. The Swedish government has set up feeding stations to save this endangered species. Further, Red Foxes are being hunted down to increase the chances of survival of the Arctic Fox.

The Scandinavian Wolf - The Scandinavian Wolf had become extinct due to overhunting in Sweden. Fortunately, around the 1980s, many wolves migrated from Finland and Russia, and their population has grown since. Wolves are banned in Northern Sweden because of the reindeer herding industry. So, most of the wolves are found in the central and southern parts of Sweden.

Moose - Moose or the European elk are found all across Sweden. The largest moose population is found in the Sarek National Park. These animals can be spotted a lot during the summer months in the forests of Central Sweden. The White Moose is a rare variety of Eurasian Elk, and these animals are mostly found in the forests of Varmland.

Great Gray Owl - Also known as the Lapland owl, this bird is the most characteristically Swedish. These birds are also endangered, thanks to the increased cutting down of old-growth forests, which provide the best nesting ground for these birds.

Brown Bears - Brown bears are found in many parts of the country. Bear encounters in Sweden are very rare because they are very shy creatures. The best way to catch a glimpse of them is to find an experienced guide who will find you a safe hiding place.

Beavers - These very large rodents were hunted to extinction during the 1800s. Their gallbladders had an important element, acetylsalicylic acid, a natural aspirin used as a painkiller (especially for headaches) in those days. Then, a few beavers from Norway were brought into Sweden, and the rodent population has since swelled.

Lynx - These shy felines are rare to spot in the wild because of their shy nature. But they are found all over Sweden, although their population is threatened by poaching as well as licensed hunting for their furs.

Sweden's Flora

Sweden is filled with beautiful plants and flowers that thrive in the cold climes, many of which have found their way into the gardens of homeowners across the world.

Smorboll - This flowering plant has a very bad odor but looks absolutely gorgeous. It smells of rotten flesh. The stunning bright-yellow flowers attract a lot of bees who are loath to pollinate them, thanks to their offensive smells. Incidentally, Smorboll plants are best pollinated by insects that do not find the odor offensive. These flowers are also called European Globe Flowers.

Mullein - Considered a weed, this beautiful plant is one of the most resilient flora in the world and can survive in the driest, coldest, and most inhospitable regions and sprout colorful flowers. During the spring season, you will find mullein in every fjord all over Sweden.

<u>Anemones</u> - This flower is unique to the province of Härjedalen in Central Sweden. These 6-petalled flowers come in different colors

The Sami of Sweden

The Sami people of Sweden are an ancient tribe indigenous to the northern parts of Scandinavia and the Kola Peninsula of Russia. In ancient times, the population and extent of Sami and their lands were much larger. However, starting from around the 1600s, they were forced to give up their land for farming and then later on for industries such as mining and forestry.

Until around the 1700s, the Sami were hunters and gatherers. As they slowly had to give up their territories, they also took up different forms of trading, and reindeer herding was one of the earliest professions that the Sami people embraced.

Today, the Sami population of Sweden is estimated to be around 20,000. They are recognized as one of the official minority communities in the country, thereby giving them special rights. Specifically, their culture, languages, and traditions are protected by law. A Sami Parliament (Sametinget) is a government agency dedicated to the welfare of the Sami people in Sweden.

The Roma in Sweden

The Roma people who originally migrated to the west from India (some were kidnapped and brought as enslaved people) came to Sweden about 500 years ago. Although the Roma population is believed to be around 50,000 in Sweden, there is no certainty as many of them are unwilling to acknowledge their Roma roots because of discrimination and prejudices. Modern-day Romanisael (Tater) Travelers are descendants of the Roma who arrived in Scandinavia about 500 years ago.

Ten Interesting Facts about Swedish Geography

1. The Aurora Borealis phenomenon takes place 100 km above the earth's surface.

2. Over 2/3rd of Sweden is covered in forests. This area is comparable to the size of the United Kingdom.

3. The country is home to more than 95 000 lakes.

4. While most of the world refers to the country as Sweden, the correct official name is the Kingdom of Sweden.

5. In addition to the three big rivers mentioned above, other rivers flowing through Sweden are Indal, Mean, Ljusnan, Lagan, Osterdal, Storuman, and Skellefteån.

6. In Sweden, Happy Hour is called "After Work."

7. The Swedes enjoy the longest life expectancy in all of Europe.

8. Nearly 300 000 to 400 000 moose roam the forests of Sweden.

9. Sweden is home to the famous Ice Hotel. It is recreated in the village of Jukkasjärvi every year using two tonnes of ice.

10. Sweden is home to the largest model of the solar system.

4. Popular Swedish Tourist Attractions

The previous three chapters would have let you know that Sweden is a country steeped in rich history and beautiful geography backed by a warm, welcoming society. Replete with stunning landscapes and vibrant culture, Sweden is one of the most tourist-friendly nations in the world.

You can visit during summer to soak in the warmth of the midnight sun or in winter to participate in majestic snow adventure sports, or come away enthralled by the brilliant colors of the Northern Lights. It is a country that offers wonderful options all through the year and for all seasons. In fact, many global travelers have given Sweden the moniker "the crown jewel of Scandinavia."

And finally, it is one of the safest countries in the world, except for petty theft and the usual scammers who target the uninitiated tourist. If you keep clear from and stay wary of such people, your travel to Sweden will be enriching and fun.

Old Town - Stockholm

Also called Old Town, this is the place where Stockholm was established way back in the 13th Century. Many medieval architectural structures are still standing in Old Town, each of them meticulously looked after. The narrow stone-paved, cobbled paths add to the old-world charm.

The main square, Stortorget, is surrounded by medieval merchant houses and several cathedrals and churches interspersed between the Royal Coin Museum, the Post Museum, and the Nobel Museum.

Drottningholm Palace

Drottningholm Palace, a UNESCO World Heritage site, is found on the island of Lovö and is also the official residence of the Swedish Royal Family. Drottningholm translates to "Queen's Islet." It dates back to the 17th Century, although it has undergone multiple renovations. The island of Lovö is about 11 km from Stockholm and is reached by ferry ride.

The fairy-tale palace and its Baroque- and English-style garden house many architectural wonders, including:

- A 17th-century Chinese Pavilion.

- Bronze sculptures from Denmark and Bohemia are all spoils of war.

- An 18th-century Palace Theater, which still holds performances during the summer. Even today, the theater continues to use the original stage machinery for performances.

- The interiors of this palace best illustrate the beauty of Rococo architecture.

The Vasa Museum - Stockholm

The Vasa Museum opened in 1990, and attracts more than a million visitors yearly. This museum houses the restructured warship Vasa, built in 1628 under the aegis of the Swedish Imperial Navy. However, the engineers who built it underestimated her weight, and the ship sank on her maiden voyage.

It remained underwater until 1961 when a successful salvage operation by the Swedish Navy under the command of Commodore Edward Clason brought up the sunken ship in April 1961. Since then, the ship has been restructured and has become a museum in its own right. It can take you an entire day to complete the tour of the Vasa museum, with 10 separate exhibitions and four other museum ships to see and explore.

The Ice Hotel and Kiruna Town

The Ice Hotel is located in Kiruna, the northernmost town of Sweden. Here, the midnight sun can be seen right from the middle of May to the middle of July. Kiruna was originally a Lapp settlement. Somewhere in the 1900s, iron ore was discovered, and slowly it turned into a mining town. Sadly, mining has resulted in subsidence, and so Kiruna town is being shifted to the foothills of Luossavaara Mountain.

The Ice Hotel has located about 17 km from Kiruna. It is recreated every year using the frozen ice from River Torne. During summer, this place is a hotspot for canoeing, river rafting, etc.

Stockholm City Hall

The Stockholm City Hall, situated on the island of Kungsholmen, was built between 1911 and 1923. Eight million bricks from the Lina Brick Factory were used for this structure. The Nobel Prize is presented every year in this building. Some interesting and important facts about Stockholm City Hall:

- The Municipal Council of Stockholm uses this building as its office, with more than 250 government offices inside it.

- The architect of the building was Ragnar Östberg.

- It has a 106-meter tall tower with three crowns at its peak. This is the national coat of arms.

The Göta Canal

The Göta Canal, built in the 19th Century, is 190 km long and is considered to be one of Sweden's engineering marvels. It connects the Trollhätte Canal and also Lakes Vänern and Vättern making it a lengthy water link right from Stockholm to Gothenburg, linking the northeast to the southwest part of Sweden. It is one of the biggest tourist attractions in the country today. Here are some fun and interesting facts about the Göta Canal:

- It took more than 22 years to build this canal. The canal was dug by hand using wooden shovels.

- It has 65 bridges and 58 locks. The first lock completed in 1813 is still in use today.

- It takes four days to travel through the entire stretch of the canal. Many cruises and passenger boats take people on a ride through the Göta Canal.

Visby Town

The walled town of Visby in Gotland is steeped in Medieval history and is filled with ruined churches. Experts opine that Visby was a center of trade and commerce around the 9th Century. It is very easy to lose yourself in this quaint town as you walk in the labyrinthine cobbled pathways of this UNESCO World Heritage Site. Some of the timber buildings that you can see here belong to the 17th and 18th centuries. The 700-year-old wall around Visby is a must-see. Some fun facts:

- Visby is one of the best-preserved UNESCO World Heritage Sites in Scandinavia.

- There are more than 200 medieval houses and buildings in Visby

- This town is accessible only by air and boat.

- The wall around this town has 44 defensive towers.

Liseberg Theme Park

Attracting over three million visitors every year, the Liseberg Theme Park is one of Sweden's most popular tourist destinations and one of the oldest in Europe. It opened in 1923. It is filled with experiences and rides for everyone, including children's carousels, adrenaline-pumping rides and roller coasters for adults, castles, bumper cars, and more.

The Big Wheel at the Liseberg Theme Park is the place for stunning 360-degree views of Gothenburg. Here are some fun facts about this amazing theme park in Sweden:

- Pink and green are the official colors of the park.

- It is one of the top 10 amusement parks in the world, according to Forbes.

- The property was named Lisas Berg (or Lisa's Mountain) by the owner, Johan Anders Lamberg, after his wife, Elisabeth Soderberg. The entire region came to be called Liseberg after that.

Öresund Bridge

The Öresund Bridge in Malmo, just a 15-minute drive from the city center, is a magnificent piece of architecture that opened in 1999. It links Sweden and Denmark and has both railways and roadways built into it. Some fun facts about this amazing bridge:

- The construction started in 1995 and was opened to traffic in 2000.

- The heads of state from Denmark and Sweden jointly conducted the opening ceremony.

  When this bridge was built, it brought many skilled artisans and workers to Malmo, which is believed to have increased innovation in the city.

- The bridge symbolizes the connection between Sweden and the rest of Europe.

Kärnan

The most prominent feature of the Swedish town of Helsingborg is the huge brick tower called "The Kernel" or Kärnan. It was constructed as a town watch tower in the 14th Century and is located in the market square. You can climb a steep wooden staircase of 190 steps inside to reach the top of the 35-meter tower and get some stunning views of the town and the surroundings, including the Öresund Bridge and Denmark's Helsingor. You can catch the ferry to Helsingor from right here.

Uppsala Cathedral

The Uppsala Cathedral, or Domkyrka, is Uppsala's most prominent and beautiful feature. Although its original construction dates back to 1270, multiple additions have been made to this cathedral. What strikes you first is the stunning

19th-century Neo-Gothic spire and brilliant glass-stained windows. Other additions made to the cathedral include:

- The Baroque pulpit was added in 1707.

- The Silver Chamber in the north tower houses a gold brocade robe worn by Queen Margaret (she lived in the 14th and 15th centuries).

Lund Cathedral

The Lund Cathedral is one of Sweden's most popular and most visited sites. The Roman architectural cathedral forms an imposing structure thanks to the magnificent twin towers. Here are some interesting facts about the Lund Cathedral:

- The original structure that stood at this place was built during the time of Danish King Canute IV around 1080. However, the current structure dates from the 12th Century.

- The crypt is the oldest part of the Lund Cathedral. The figures carved on the roof are that of Finn, a mythical giant believed to have built this cathedral.

- The magnificently carved reredos overlooking the main altar is from the 14th Century.

Sigtuna

Sigtuna is believed to be Sweden's first town, founded in 980 CE. This idyllic town is situated along the banks of Lake Mälaren (overlooking Skaven Bay) and just a 45-minute car ride away from Stockholm. The history of the town is palpable as it seeps out of the numerous medieval rune stones, cathedrals, and other structures that dot the town.

It is a very small and sparsely populated town, and even until the 19th Century, just about 600 people were living there. The sudden spurt in the population (about 50,000 now) is because of the Stockholm Arlanda Airport, built in the latter half of the 20th Century.

Abisko National Park

Situated in the Swedish province of Lapland, where there is 24-hour sunlight for many weeks in summer, Abisko National Park is about 77 square km in area and is filled with Nordic wildlife, flora, and fauna. The National Park was established in 1909. However, the Sami people have lived here for thousands of years. Its pristine natural beauty makes it one of the most attractive tourist destinations in Sweden.

People visit here during the winter for winter adventures and, during the summer, for long hikes through the natural beauty. The Abisko National Park is situated within the Arctic Circle, where the chances of sighting the Aurora Borealis are very high. The Abisko National Park was set up to preserve the Nordic wild and also for scientific research.

Sarek National Park

Sarek National Park is also situated in the province of Lapland and is the most mountainous region in the entire country. It holds six of the 13 Swedish peaks and is home to about 100 glaciers. This place was the primary shooting location for the 2017 film, "The Ritual."

Sarek National Park is home to many elks and predators too. The Sami people have lived here for thousands of years, and even today, they have the right to use the forest resources for their needs, with the exception of hunting elks which is banned.

Ten Interesting Facts to Know before Your Travel to Sweden

1. Sweden takes cleanliness very, very seriously. It is one of the cleanest countries in the world.

2. Sweden has one of the highest tax rates in the world. The standard VAT rate is presently 25%.

3. Sweden has the highest number of McDonald's restaurants in all of Europe.

4. Sweden has the highest number of patents in all of Europe. The most famous patents are the pacemaker, tetrapak, and dynamite.

5. The Swedes are known for their generosity and charitable nature. It is the only country in the world where donations are more than 1% of its GDP.

6. Sweden is one of the most progressive nations in the world, leading the way in LGBTQ rights.

7. The Swedes love their coffee, and the country tops the list of the most coffee drinkers in the world.

8. The Swedish monarchy dates back a thousand years.

9. King Eric III became a successful pirate after he was forced to give up the throne.

10. Sweden is so good with recycling that it
imports waste from other countries.

5. Swedish Quiz

After finishing the book, answer these trivia questions to test yourself. You can use them for a party quiz as well. What better than a quiz to conclude this book on Swedish trivia!

Questions

1. Pressure tactics work very well in Swedish business environments. (True/False)

2. What is the meaning of Varsågod?

3. What are the two most important summer festivals celebrated in Sweden?

4. Religion is enforced by the Swedish government. (True/False)

5. What is the meaning of "Folkhemmet?"

6. Who were the most famous people in Sweden, and when did their prosperity peak?

7. What ended the Kalmar Union?

8. Who is considered Sweden's founding father?

9. What treaty, along with the Copenhagen Treaty, resulted in setting the boundaries

of modern-day Sweden, Denmark, and Norway?

10. Which is the first country to introduce the Freedom to Press and Information Act?

11. Which are the three primary rivers of Sweden?

12. What is the official language of Sweden? Can you get by with English in the country?

13. What is the name of the mountain range in Sweden that is part of the Scandinavian Mountains?

14. When did Stockholm become the capital of Sweden?

15. Which are the four largest lakes in Sweden?

16. When was Gamla Stan or the Old Town in Stockholm established?

17. Where is the Drottningholm Palace located?

18. At which of its voyages did the Vasa warship sink?

19. How often is the Ice Hotel in Kiruna recreated?

20. How long is the Gota Canal?

Answers

1. False. The Swedes are objective, non-emotional people for whom pressure tactics or emotional appeals will not work.

2. Varsågod is a Swedish term that is used in different contexts, such as to say "please," "will be so kind as to…" etc.

3. Valborg, a community festival heralding the start of warm, sunny weather, and Midsummer, a celebration of the summer solstice.

4. False. The state and religion are separate in secular Sweden.

5. Folkhemmet means "a country household" and is a term that symbolizes equality and dignity for all its citizens, regardless of caste, creed, gender, race, etc.

6. The Vikings are the most famous people in Sweden who were at the top of their game between 800 and 1050 CE.

7. The Stockholm Bloodbath.

8. Gustav Vasa.

9. The Treaty of Roskilde

10. Sweden, in 1658

11. Rivers Ume, Torne, and the Angerman

12. Swedish is the official language of the Swedes. Yes, you can get by with English in the country. However, it is best to learn Swedish if you want to become a Swede.

13. Kolen Mountains

14. 1523

15. The four largest lakes in Sweden are Hjälmaren, Malaren, Vanern, and Vattern.

16. In the 13th Century.

17. On the island of Lovo.

18. On its maiden voyage.

19. Every year.

20. It is 190 km long, connecting Stockholm to Gothenburg.

Conclusion

Sweden ranks high on the world's list of nations offering a dignified, happy life with equal opportunities to all of its citizens. It is a country anyone would be proud to call their home. Further, it is heaven for tourists seeking adventure, stunning offbeat locations, and excellent food. The country is filled with medieval cities and towns, with quaint ancient buildings and churches still standing amidst the meandering cobbled pathways.

Learning about this beautiful, happy country is one of the best ways you can befriend it and its warming, friendly people. You can use this book to build your trivia knowledge and learn more about this country before you set out on an adventure-filled holiday there.

Sweden is filled with picturesque islands, gorgeous hiking trails, historic cities and towns, storybook fjords, verdant forests replete with unique flora and fauna, the spectacular, elusive Northern Lights, and much more. All of this is peopled by some of the most generous, gracious hosts you can meet and make friends with.

Here's one more interesting fact about Sweden before we conclude the book:

Did you know that North Korea owes Sweden SEK (Swedish Krona) 2.7 billion to Sweden for 1000 Volvo cars purchased way back in 1974?

Thanks you for reading!

One last word from the author

Of all the books to choose from, thank you very much for choosing this trivia book and reading all the way to the end!

In the introduction, I ask you why you should spend your time on this book, and I hope the content in the book can answer that question for itself!

If you think the book has lived up to your expectations (or more), you are welcome to write that in a review. Likewise, if you thought the book contained only things you could have easily found on Google or YouTube, I'd love to know!

What to read next: If you enjoyed this book, check out the other books in the Scandinavia Trivia Series here!

References

"10 Most Beautiful Lakes in Sweden." Touropia, www.touropia.com/lakes-in-sweden/.

"10 Reasons Why Trivia Is Good for You." Cerebrum Publishing, April 16 2022, cerebrumpublishing.com/10-reasons-why-trivia-is-good-for-you/.

"12 Interesting Facts about Sweden You Should Know Before Visiting | Beelinguapp Blog." Beelinguapp.com, beelinguapp.com/blog/12-interesting-facts-about-sweden.

admin. "What Are the Languages Spoken in Sweden?" ETS, February 19 2021, etranslationservices.com/languages/what-are-the-languages-spoken-in-sweden/.

AFS-USA. "Sweden: Exploring Swedish Culture | Learn with AFS-USA." AFS-USA, 2022, www.afsusa.org/countries/sweden/.

Author Andrew Helling. "Is Sweden Safe to Visit in 2022? | Safety Concerns | Travellers." Travellersworldwide.com, travellersworldwide.com/is-sweden-safe-to-visit/.

Commisceo Global. "Sweden - Language, Culture, Customs and Etiquette." Commisceo-Global.com, 2014, www.commisceo-global.com/resources/country-guides/sweden-guide.

"Did You Know- 25 Fun & Interesting Facts about Stockholm and Sweden." Nordic Experience, January 23 2018, www.nordicexperience.com/know-25-fun-interesting-facts-stockholm-sweden/.

"Freedom of the Press Act of 1766 | Swedish Legislation." Encyclopedia Britannica, www.britannica.com/topic/Freedom-of-the-Press-Act-of-1766.

"Gota Canal." Www.asce.org, www.asce.org/about-civil-engineering/history-and-heritage/historic-landmarks/gota-canal. Accessed December 25 2022.

Kamann, Matthias. "History of Sweden - 17 Most Important Events." Hej Sweden, 2 Feb. 2021, hejsweden.com/en/history-of-sweden/.

Lund University. "Swedish Culture and Traditions." Lunduniversity.lu.se, 2021, www.lunduniversity.lu.se/about-university/visit-lund-university/swedish-culture-and-traditions.

Matthias Kamann. "How Swedes Celebrate Christmas - Swedish "Jul" Traditions - Hej Sweden." Hej Sweden, 22 Feb. 2017, hejsweden.com/en/swedes-celebrate-christmas/.

"Midsummer in Sweden – a Cherished Tradition."
Visitsweden.com, visitsweden.com/what-to-
do/culture-history-and-art/swedish-
traditions/midsummer-tradition/midsummer/.

museer, Statens maritima och transporthistoriska.
"The Salvage." Www.vasamuseet.se,
www.vasamuseet.se/en/explore/vasa-
history/salvage.

Nikel, David. "17 Fascinating Facts about the
Northern Lights." Life in Norway, November 1
2020, www.lifeinnorway.net/northern-lights-
facts/.

---. "21 Fun Facts about Stockholm, Sweden."
Life in Norway, June 20 2022,
www.lifeinnorway.net/stockholm-facts/.

Riksdagsförvaltningen. "The History of the
Riksdag." Riksdagen.se, 2015,
www.riksdagen.se/en/how-the-riksdag-
works/democracy/the-history-of-the-riksdag/.

---. "What Does the Riksdag Do?" Riksdagen.se,
2015, www.riksdagen.se/en/How-the-Riksdag-
works/What-does-the-Riksdag-do/.

"Roma in Sweden: A Nation Questions Itself."
BBC News, December 4 2013,
www.bbc.com/news/magazine-25200449.

"Sami in Sweden." Sweden.se, February 22 2019,
sweden.se/life/people/sami-in-sweden.

says, Chris Fendler. "11 Fascinating Facts about
Sweden." Life in Norway, June 5 2019,
www.lifeinnorway.net/sweden-facts/.

"Schools Encouraged to Adopt "No-Shoes
Policy" to Improve Pupils' Learning and
Behaviour." The Independent, May 24 2016,
www.independent.co.uk/news/education/educati
on-news/schools-encouraged-to-adopt-noshoes-
policy-to-improve-pupils-learning-and-behaviour-
a7044576.html.

Scroope, Chara. "Swedish Culture - Core
Concepts." Cultural Atlas, 2017,
culturalatlas.sbs.com.au/swedish-culture/swedish-
culture-core-concepts.

"Sweden." Geography, March 21. 2014,
kids.nationalgeographic.com/geography/countries
/article/sweden.

"Sweden Celebrates 200 Years of Peace." The
Local Sweden, August 15 2014,
www.thelocal.se/20140815/sweden-celebrates-
200-years-of-peace/.

Swedish Institute. "Sweden and Migration."
Sweden.se, September 7 2021,
sweden.se/culture/history/sweden-and-migration.

---. "The Swedish School System." Sweden.se, May 11 2015, sweden.se/life/society/the-swedish-school-system.

"Swedish Society." Sweden.se, sweden.se/life/society.

"Swedish Weather and Climate." Visitsweden.com, February 26 2021, visitsweden.com/about-sweden/weather-and-climate/.

"The 7 Most Amazing Peaks in Sweden | Komoot." Komoot, www.komoot.com/guide/232993/peaks-in-sweden.

"Top 10 Interesting Facts about Drottningholm Palace." Discover Walks Blog, September 7 2022, www.discoverwalks.com/blog/stockholm/top-10-interesting-facts-about-drottningholm-palace/.

"Varsågud a Polite Phrase with Many Meanings." Al Johnsons Swedish Restaurant Butik, www.aljohnsonsshop.com/blog/varsgud-a-polite-phrase-with-many-meanings

"Why You Should Lose Your Shoes like a Swede." The Local Sweden, February 9 2017, www.thelocal.se/20170209/why-you-should-lose-your-shoes-like-a-swede/.

"WildSweden - Wildlife Adventures in Sweden."
WildSweden - Wildlife Adventures in Sweden,
2019, www.wildsweden.com/about/11-incredible-
images-of-swedens-wildlife.

professional before attempting any techniques outlined in this book.

By reading this document, the reader agrees that under no circumstances is the author responsible for any losses, direct or indirect, which are incurred as a result of the use of information contained within this document, including, but not limited to, —errors, omissions, or inaccuracies.

www.ingramcontent.com/pod-product-compliance
Lightning Source LLC
LaVergne TN
LVHW090220180726

843492LV00012B/2563